AMERICA NEEDS A WOMAN PRESIDENT

AMERICA
NEEDS
A
WOMAN
PRESIDENT

WORDS BY BRETT BEVELL
DRAWINGS BY EBEN DODD

MONKFISH BOOK PUBLISHING COMPANY
RHINEBECK, NEW YORK

Poem: *America Needs A Woman President* copyright © Brett Bevell, 2007
Drawings for *America Needs A Woman President* copyright © Eben Dodd, 2007
Printed in The United States of America. No part of this book may be used or reproduced in any manner without written permission from the publisher except in the case of brief quotations embodied in critical articles and reviews.
For information contact Monkfish Book Publishing Company,
27 Lamoree Road, Rhinebeck, New York 12572

ISBN: 978-0-9766843-5-0

Library of Congress Cataloging-in-Publication-Data pending:
Please contact the publisher for more information.

Monkfish Book Publishing Company
27 Lamoree Road
Rhinebeck, New York 12572
www.monkfishpublishing.com

For Helema, and all women working to create peace on Earth.

Acknowledgements:

I wish to offer my deep gratitude to Paige Kitson, who introduced my work to
Lama Surya Das
And to Lama Surya Das, for suggesting that I write this book.

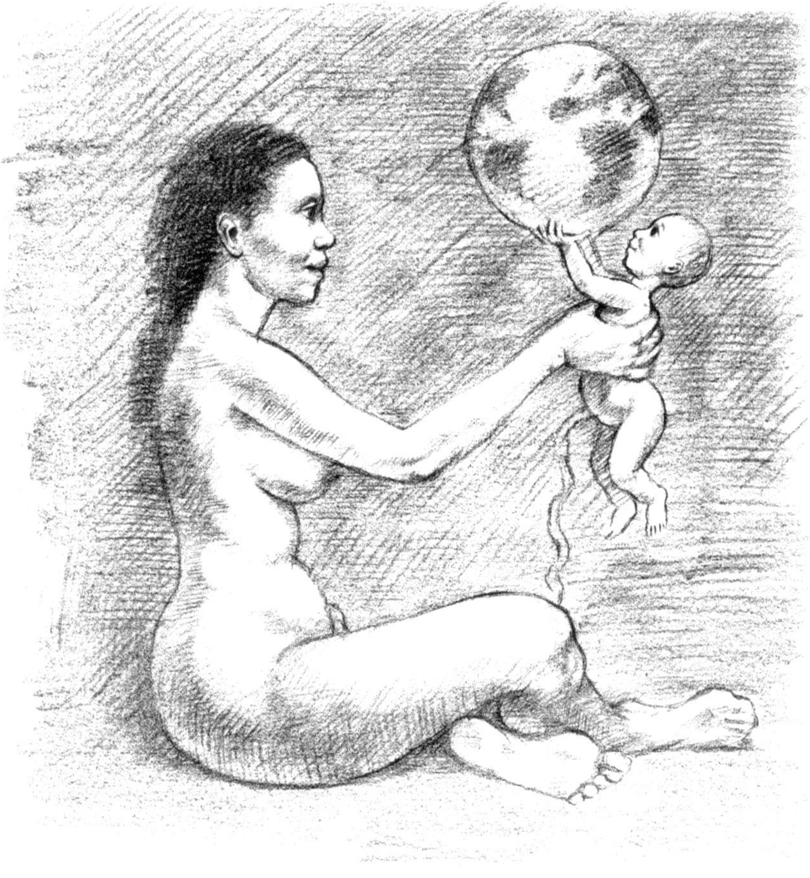

AMERICA NEEDS
A WOMAN PRESIDENT
GIVING BIRTH
TO A NEW AMERICA
EMBRACING THE WORLD

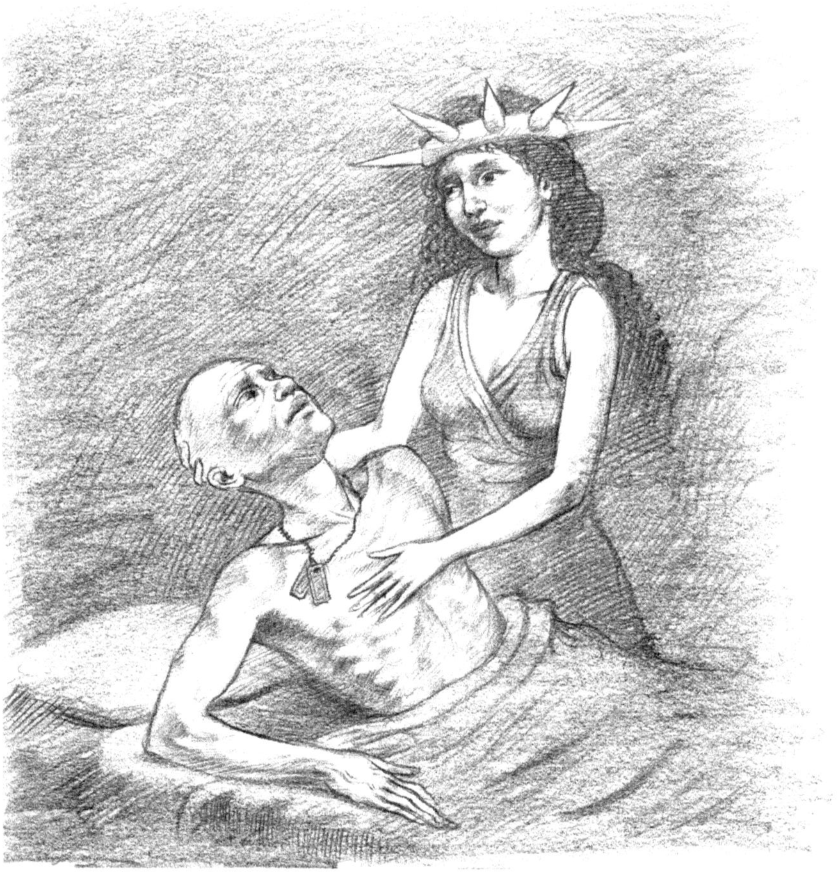

America needs
A woman President
Open hearted compassion is
Her greatest family value

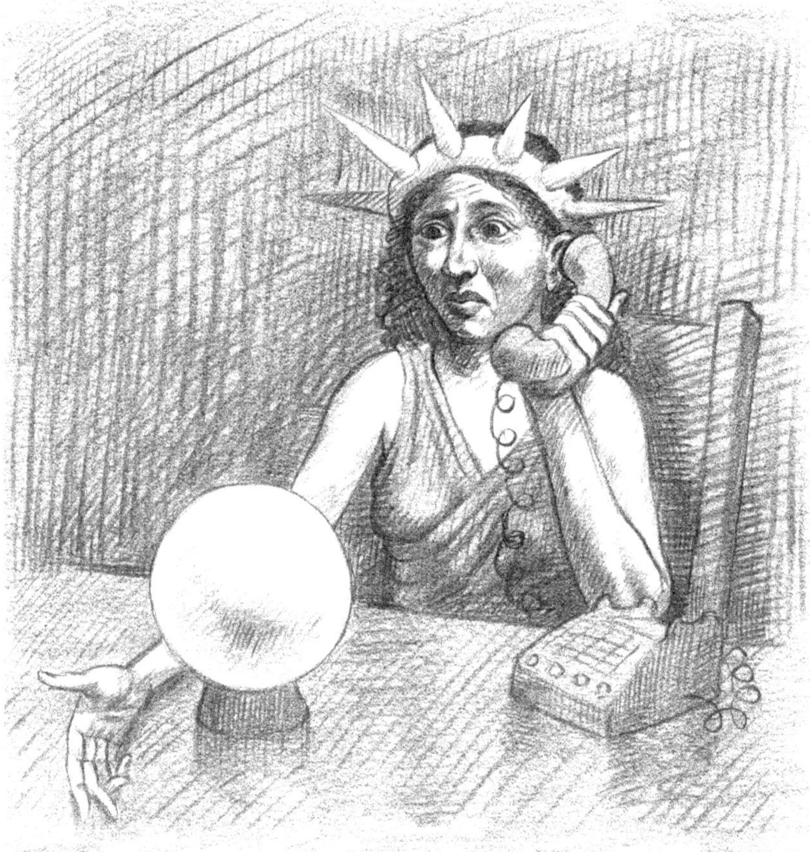

An intuitive President
Who can feel if
The information is true
Before sending troops
To war

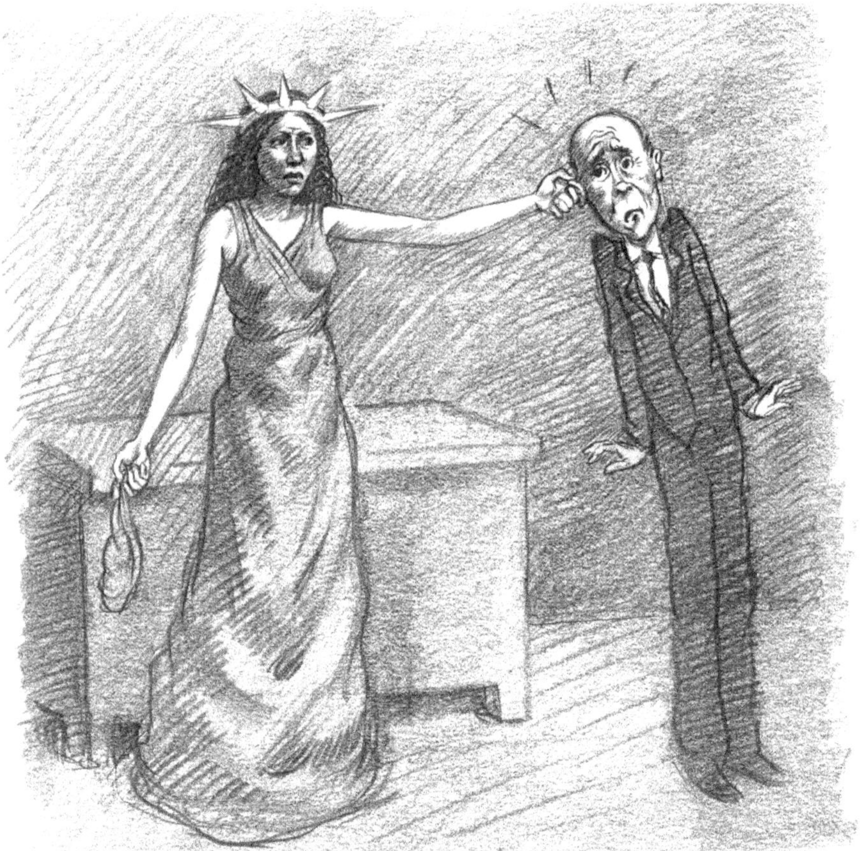

America needs
A woman President
Scrubbing ears of advisors
So they hear with their
Hearts not statistics

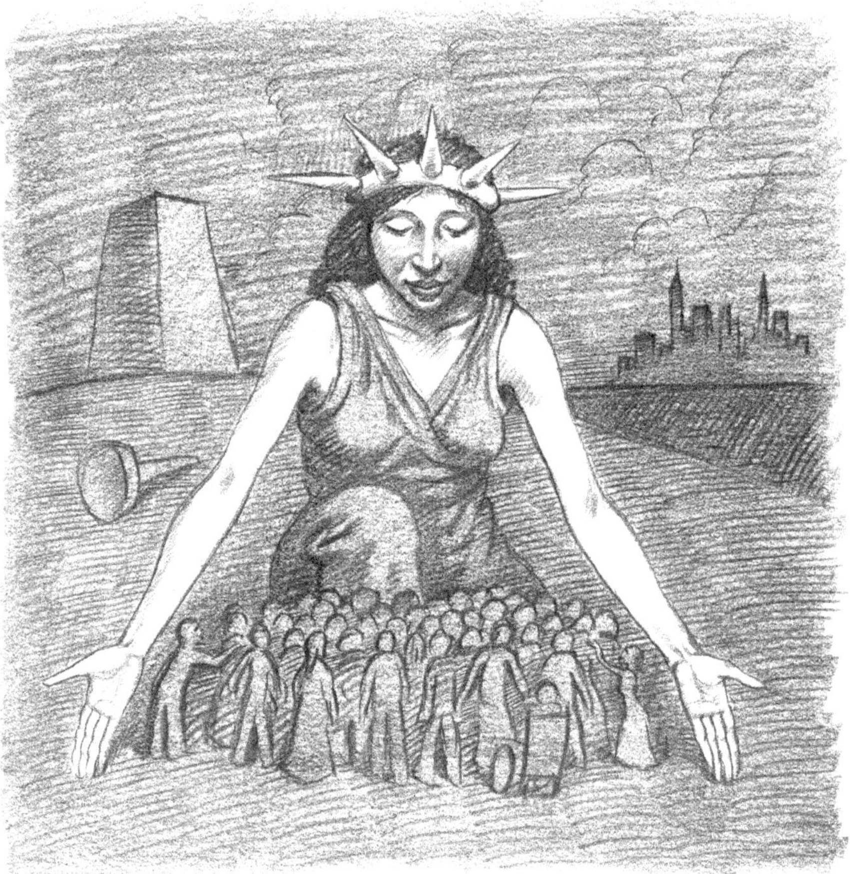

America needs
A Goddess in office
Statue of Liberty
Who will care for the
Poor and huddled masses

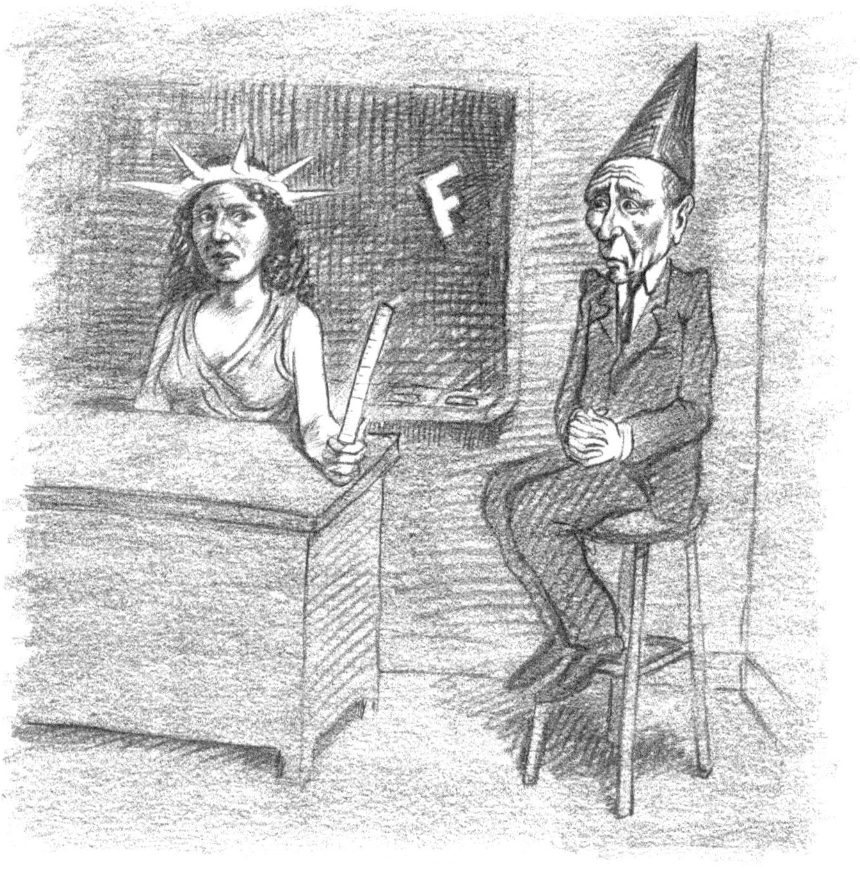
F

A teacher President
Who can read between the
Lines of nafta and gatt
And will grade
Bully corporations accordingly

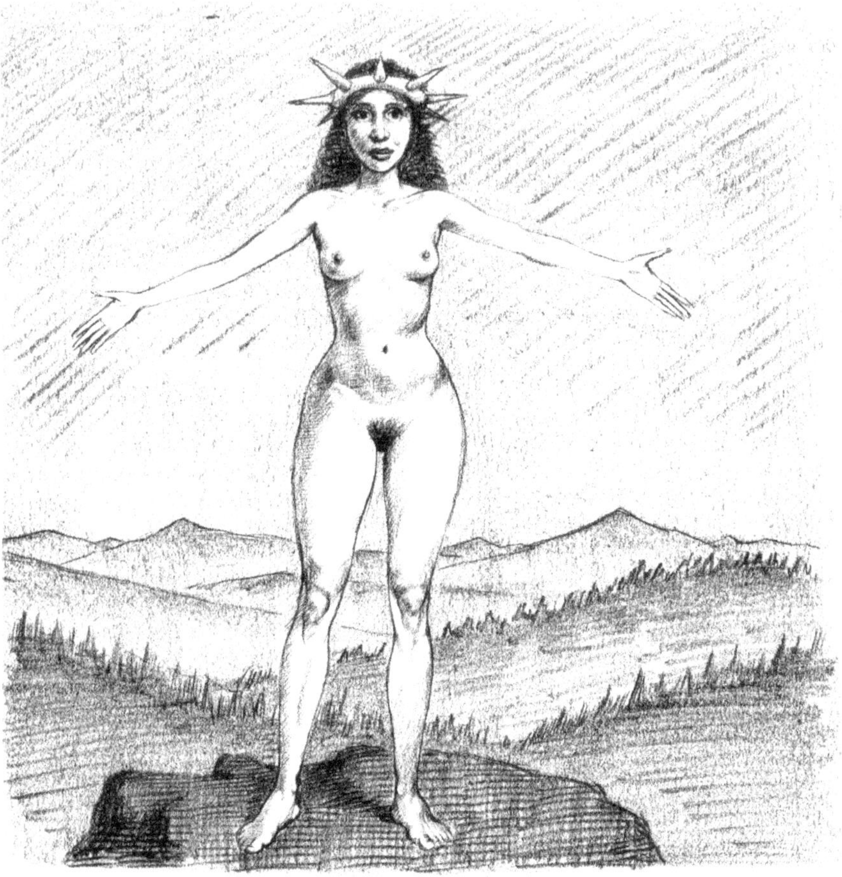

A MAIDEN PRESIDENT
WHO ACKNOWLEDGES
ALL LIFE
WITH SUPREME REVERENCE
BEYOND BORDERS, COLORS OR
RELIGION

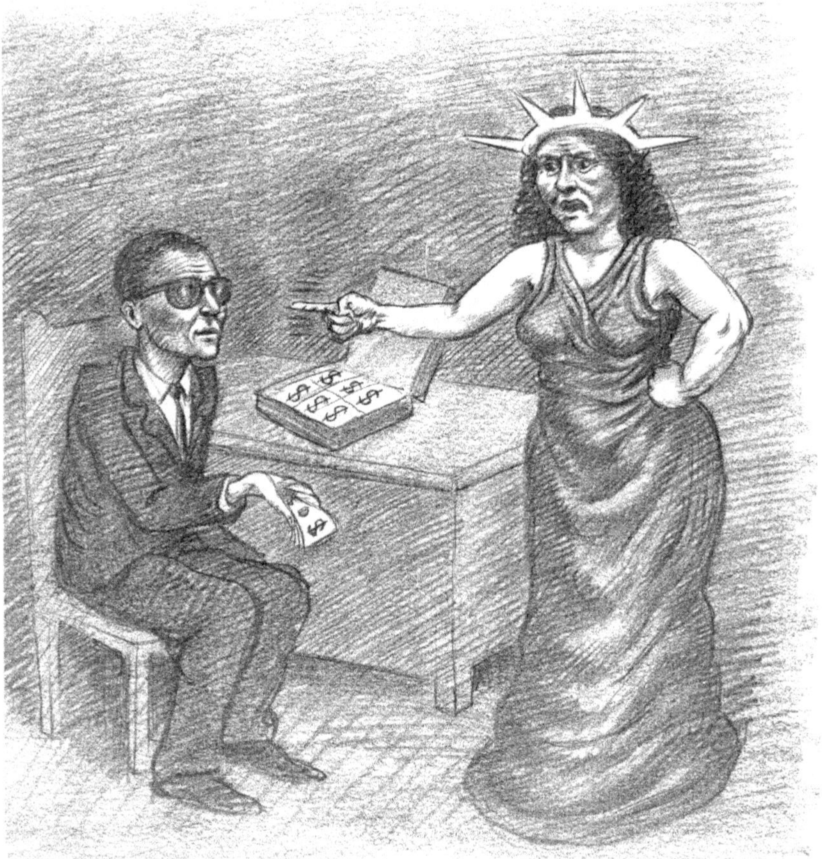

America needs
A menopausal President
Unafraid to speak
Her mind
Without quivering
To special interests

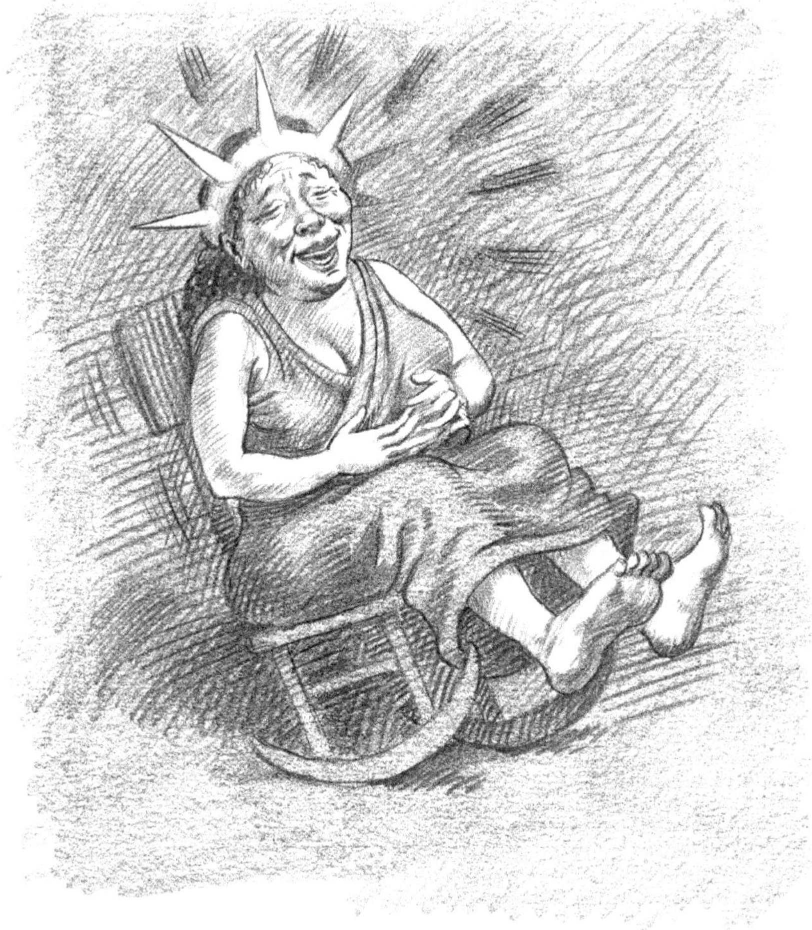

A GRANDMOTHER PRESIDENT
WISE WOMAN
WHO ADMITS PAST MISTAKES
WITH GREAT LAUGHTER

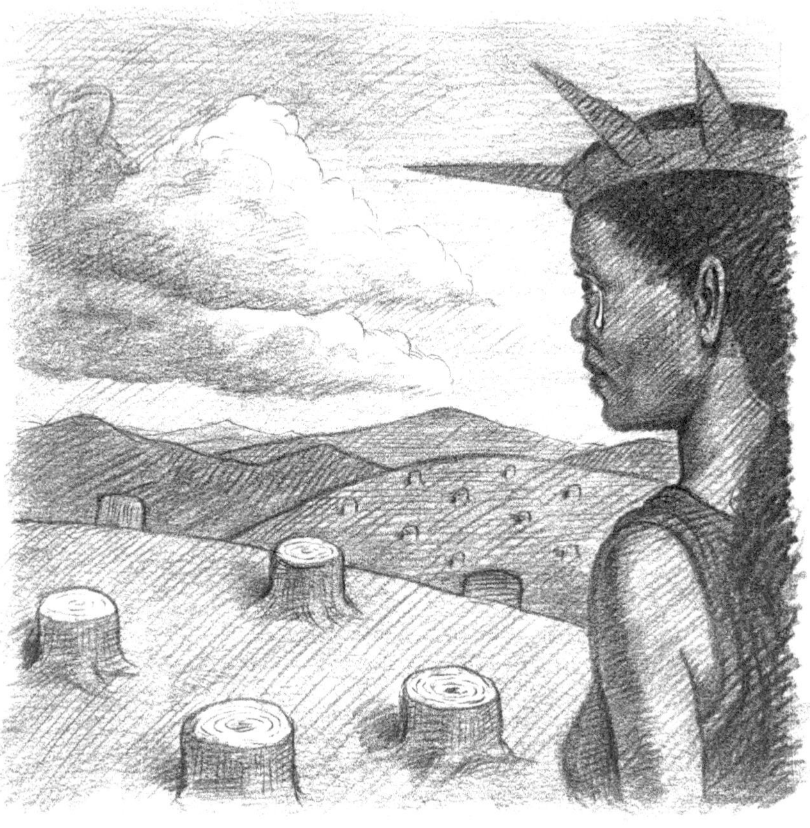

America needs
A woman President
Who can cry
At what we've done
To our forests

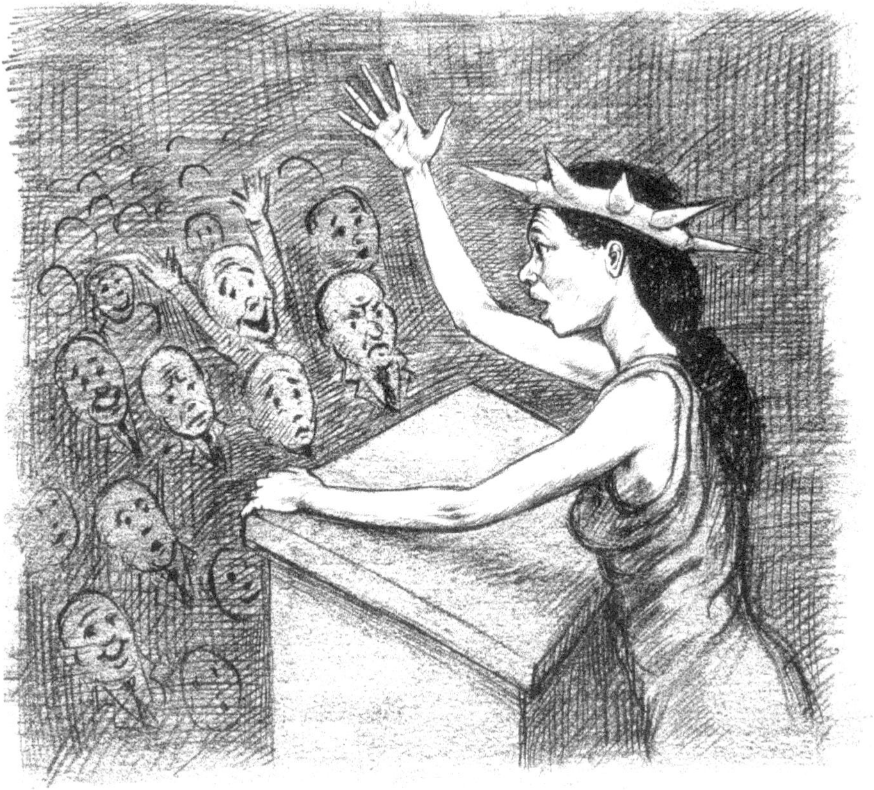

America needs
A priestess President
Enchanting Congress
With her speeches
Restoring those liberties lost
In the wasteland of fear

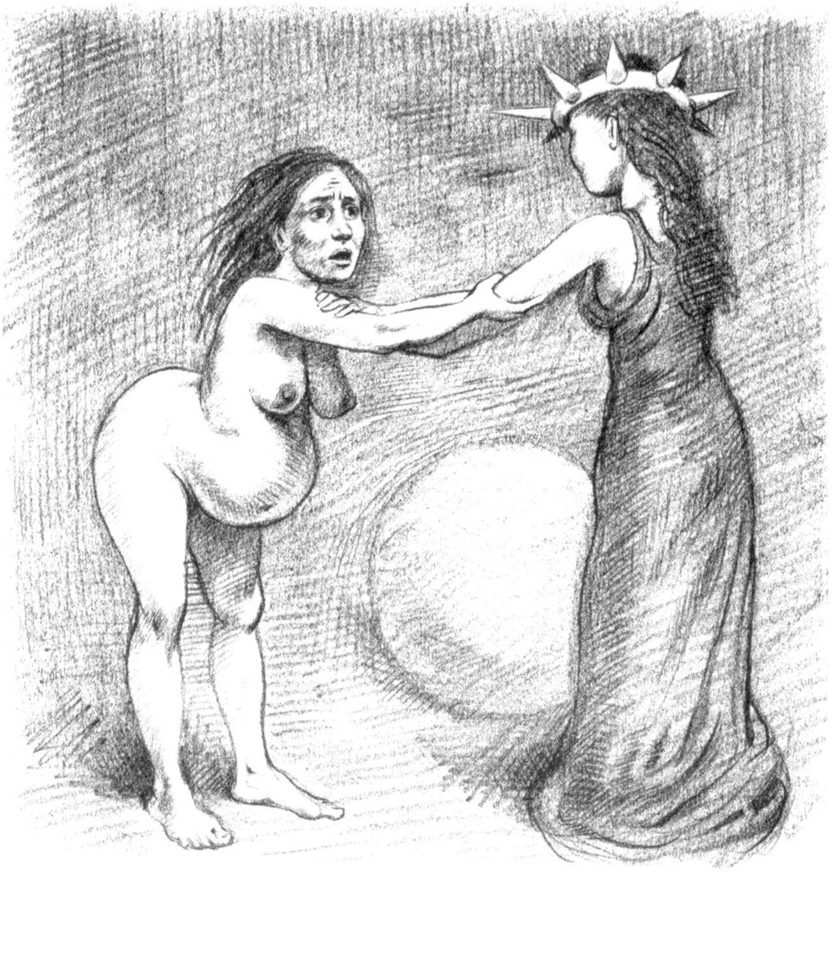

A mid-wife President
Who will teach us
How to breathe
During times of new birth
That are painful

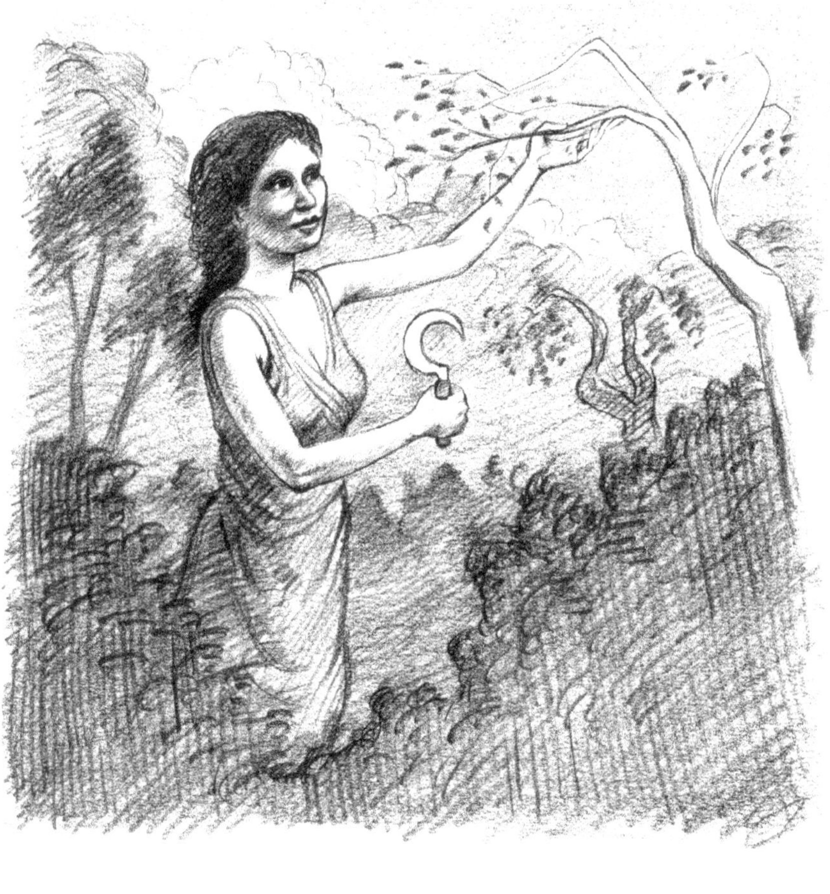

An herbalist President
Drawing strength
From natures goodness
And offering
Free health care to all

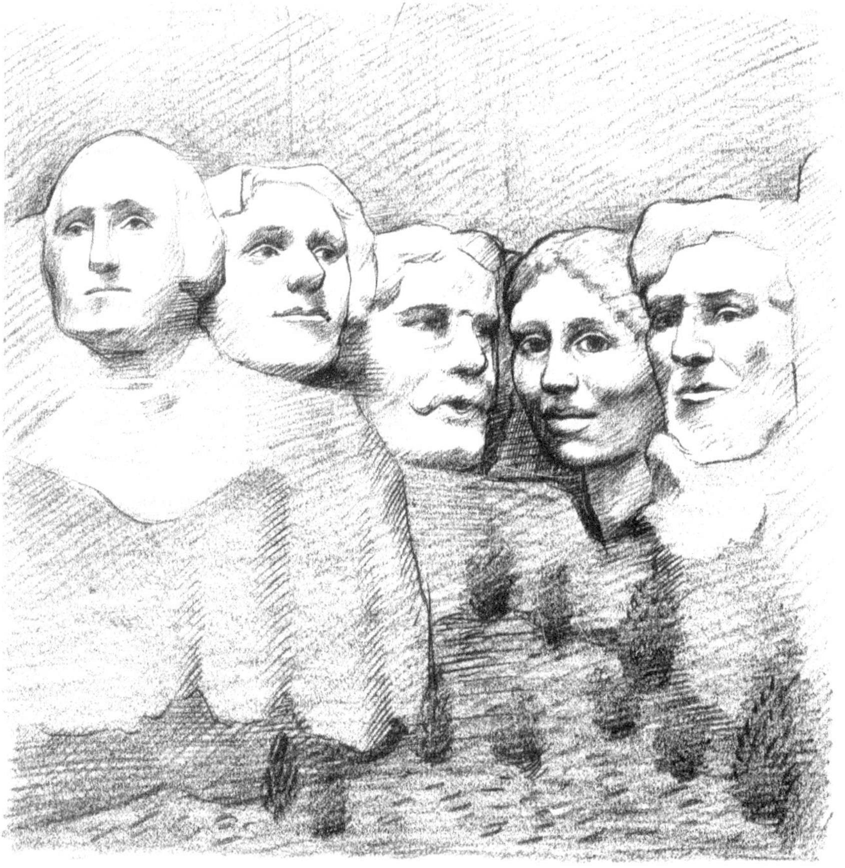

A medicine woman President
Who can see
With the eyes of Earth
And holds counsel
With her ancestors

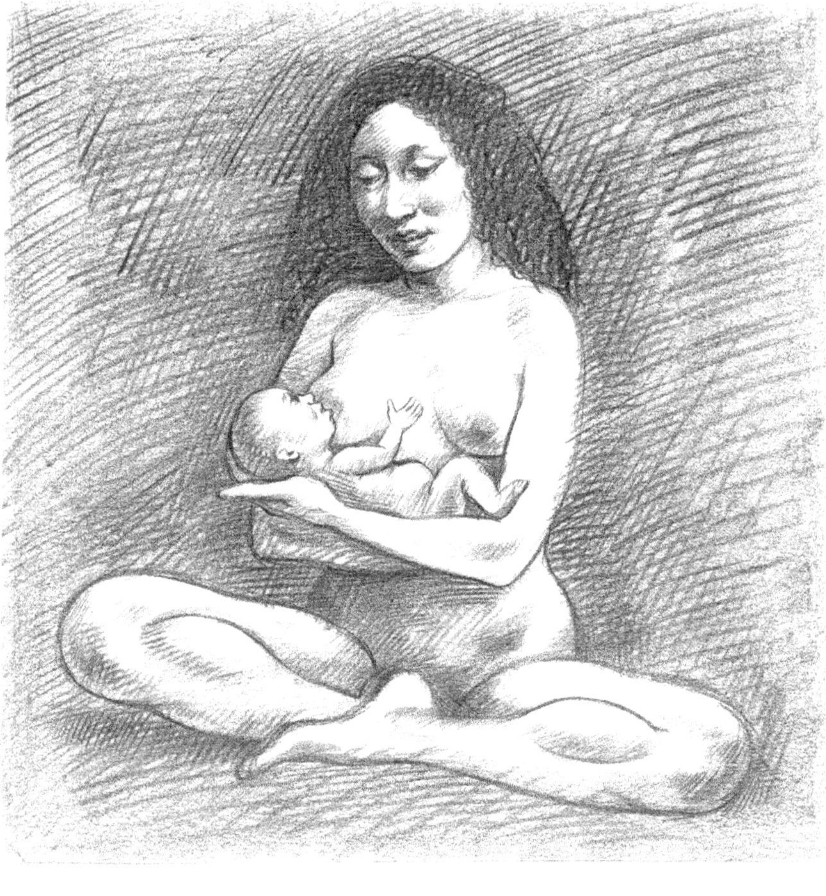

AMERICA NEEDS
A WOMAN PRESIDENT
AWARE OF HER POWER
TO NURTURE

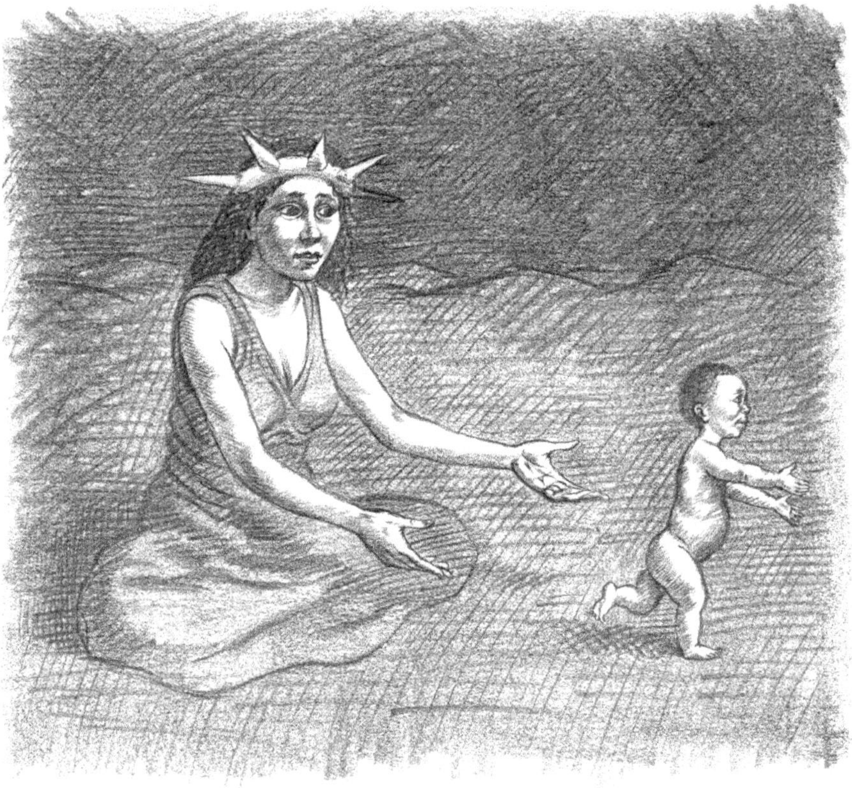

A MOTHER PRESIDENT
WHO UNDERSTANDS
THE CYCLES OF LIFE
AND LETS GO

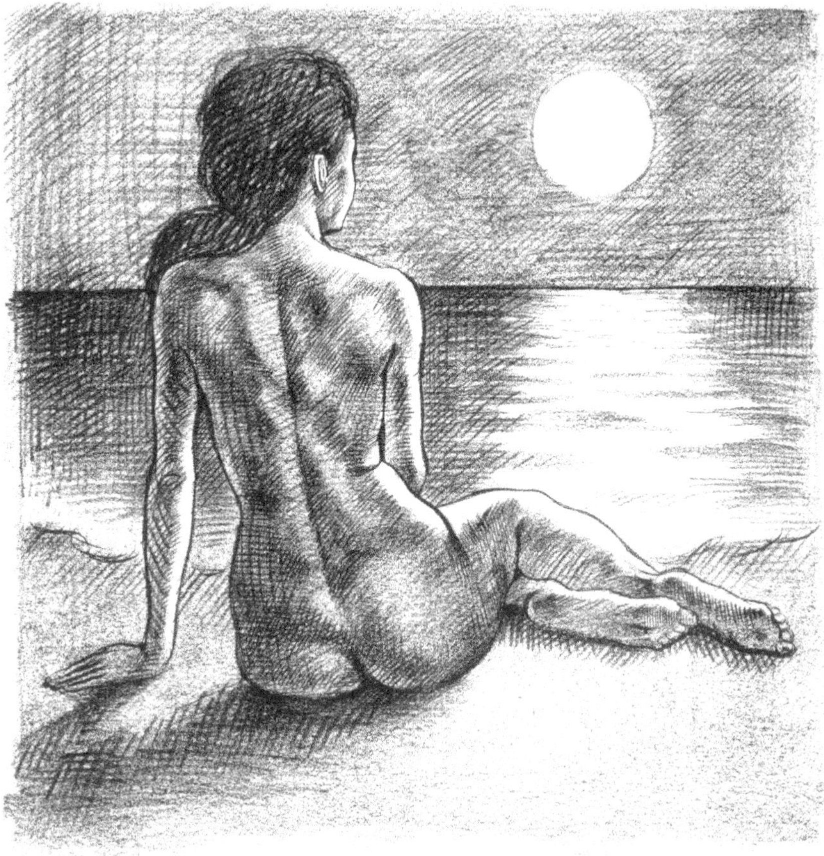

AMERICA NEEDS
A WOMAN PRESIDENT
WHO TRUSTS
IN THE WISDOM OF THE MOON

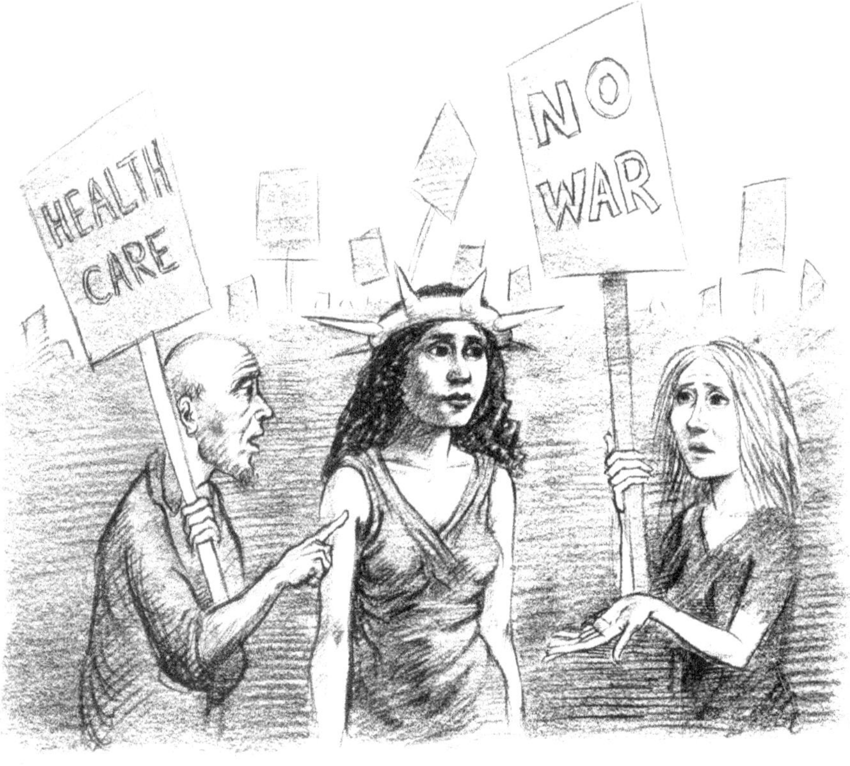

HEALTH CARE
NO WAR

AMERICA NEEDS
A WOMAN PRESIDENT
WHO CAN LISTEN
WHEN OTHERS ARE SPEAKING

BRETT BEVELL IS THE AUTHOR OF SEVERAL BOOKS, INCLUDING *AMERICA NEEDS A BUDDHIST PRESIDENT,* AND *AMERICA NEEDS A WOMAN PRESIDENT.* HE HAS ELECTRIFIED AUDIENCES AROUND THE WORLD WITH HIS MASTERFUL LIVE ORAL RECITATIONS, AND HAS OFTEN BEEN COMPARED TO THE LATE POET ALLEN GINSBERG. HIS POETRY IS FEATURED ON SEVERAL CDS AND IS PART OF NPR'S PERMANENT WEBSITE ARCHIVES. HE IS ALSO WINNER OF THE 1995 PAUL LAURANCE DUNBAR POETRY PRIZE. BRETT TEACHES WRITING WORKSHOPS AT THE OMEGA INSTITUTE IN RHINEBECK, NEW YORK AND AT ALEX GREY'S CHAPEL OF THE SACRED MIRRORS IN NEW YORK CITY.

EBEN DODD IS AN ARTIST LIVING IN OAKLAND, CA. SINCE MOVING TO THE BAY AREA IN 1999, HE HAS BEEN EXHIBITING DRAWINGS AND PAINTINGS IN GALLERIES ON THE WEST COAST. PREVIOUSLY, HIS WORK APPEARED IN *WW3 ILLUSTRATED MAGAZINE.* THIS IS HIS SECOND COLLABORATION WITH BRETT BEVELL; THE FIRST WAS *AMERICA NEEDS A BUDDHIST PRESIDENT.*

"Brett Bevel is evocative, eloquent. A man in balance with his own deep feminine, he inspires a new America whose leaders embody true wisdom and wholeness. *America Needs A Woman President* strikes a poignant beat whose message cuts to the very heart of our nation's repressed potential."

Llyn Roberts, M.A.
Author of *The Good Remembering*
and co-author of *Shamanic Reiki*

"What the world needs is more men like Brett Bevell whose inspiring poetry calls out for the leadership of women to help solve some of the worlds most profound problems. His gift for language celebrates women's capacities and contributions with a power that lifts us all. "

Carla Goldstein, Director of the Women's Institute at Omega

"Brett's poetry is a cry out to the global citizen...to remember our humanity and compassion, and to celebrate our communities and our abilities (and responsibilities!) to create change."

Kavitha Rao, co-founder of Common Fire Foundation
and an active member of The Fellowship of **Reconciliation**,
an organization dedicated to interfaith peace activism.

"Brett's worshipful invocation of a "Goddess in Office" proposes a government based on wisdom and compassion, describing qualities we'd like to expect from a world leader — whether or not we throw our vote to the first presidential candidate in a skirt."

Visionary Artists **Alex & Allyson Grey**
Co-founders of The Chapel of The Sacred Mirrors

"Brett Bevel makes an eloquent and passionate plea for sanity in *America Needs a Woman President*. Truer words were never written, nor been so timely. America absolutely does need a woman president — before it is too late."

Donna Henes, author of *The Queen of My Self*

www.ingramcontent.com/pod-product-compliance
Lightning Source LLC
Chambersburg PA
CBHW021006050525
26180CB00014B/53
9780976684350